FUGITIVE,
in Full View

Also by Jack Marshall

FUGITIVE,
in Full View

JACK MARSHALL

Coffee House Press
Minneapolis
2017

Coffee House Press books are available to the trade through our primary distributor, Consortium Book Sales & Distribution, cbsd.com or (800) 283-3572. For personal orders, catalogs, or other information, write to info@coffeehousepress.org.

Coffee House Press is a nonprofit literary publishing house. Support from private foundations, corporate giving programs, government programs, and generous individuals helps make the publication of our books possible. We gratefully acknowledge their support in detail in the back of this book.

LIBRARY OF CONGRESS CATALOGING-IN-PUBLICATION DATA

Names: Marshall, Jack, 1936– author.
Title: Fugitive, in full view / Jack Marshall.
Description: Minneapolis : Coffee House Press, 2017.
Identifiers: LCCN 2016045338 | ISBN 9781566894692 (paperback)
Subjects: | BISAC: POETRY / American / General.
Classification: LCC PS3563.A722 A6 2017 | DDC 811/.54—dc23
LC record available at https://lccn.loc.gov/2016045338

Acknowledgments

The cover image, "Merging Clusters in 30 Doradus," is public domain and courtesy of NASA, ESA, and E. Sabbi.

Some of the poems in this book previously appeared in *Slate, Serving House Journal, Contemporary World Literature, Poetry Flash,* and *Redwood Coast Review.* "Bird, Are You Still" was published as a broadside by Tangram Press, and "What the Sky Collects" in the One (More) Glass series from Gerald, Michaela, and Bernie Fleming.

PRINTED IN THE UNITED STATES OF AMERICA
24 23 22 21 20 19 18 17   1 2 3 4 5 6 7 8

For Naomi, David, Aaron, Natie,
and in memory of
Allan Kornblum and Steve Kowit

Contents

SECTION 6

SECTION 7

FUGITIVE,
in Full View

Ignition

Reaching eighty, mouthing on,
call it ego, call it Nietzsche's
"optimism of a desperado,"
fugitive, in full view,
ignition near at hand
needs a mouth to bloom.

The book begins, the pages
blank, white, witless,
lit beams hover
before flitting away.

Boo-hoo does no good;
not a jot registers on the
Richter scale. Good-bye,
hello, the end is back, gotta go
perishable, virtual, wormhole book.

SECTION 1

Aleppo Winter

Horses, in their stalls
That families hide in, feed on more
Than children will,

And homesickness worsens horror
Of the present to yearning for their past
Apprehension but less terror.

I remember my mother saying, for her as a girl
Aleppo winters were like being caught in a river
Rising and night growing cold as marble

Freezing you in place,
And every place in you was everywhere
Ice. She liked her talk like her cooking, spiced.

When I once asked why she always expected
The worst: "I don't expect the worst,"
She said, "I expect the expected."

Memory's meat
We eat and keep
Repeating.

Decades later, reading in Malaparte's *Kaputt*
Of a winter night in farthest Finland,
German's shelling sent a mass flight

Into the lake, the heavy guns driving them on
The very night the lake freezes over.
Soon all fixed in place, a thousand

Frozen faces as if sliced clean by an ax
Caught in last living grimaces of terror and torment—
On Lake Ladoga's vast sheet of white marble rested

A thousand cavalry horses'
Heads stuck out of the crust
Of ice.

A New Kind of Mind

There are days with no other way
than going out to meet sun, leaf, shadow,
not to hew memory's sugar cube

into marble or dissolve it, licked
clean by forgetting, but to feel on the skin
the warmth of sunshine others see in.

Towering, seagulls slide, whose eyes notice
what is lost to those who go
by feeling close to the ground

where eyes look forward, memory back,
as if an open doorway revives the eye
to unforeseen happiness that lights

a new kind of mind: no hewn marble,
but possibility's aura where none was before,
like a seeing-eye dog pawing at the door.

Love, and Leftovers

More often than I can make visible
to her; more often than she is near or
present, she becomes by making real

her happiness for all around: her look, direct;
intention, clear; inner complexity
richer, like her laugh; her hunches quick,

intricate, too subtle for spelling and necessary
to their turning out right.
More tender growing older

tenderizes the delicate parts, even
assuming our failures return, able like us
of doing over, having the luxury of later.

Mistakes, repeated, become habits;
insomniacs can bait sleep with gravy—
soaked dollar bills for all they're worth

in the schools of the new stampede,
enclosed serenity, knowing all
and at once the new astonishment saving

no expense at being true. I am calling then
on whatever powers may steer us
to love, and leftovers, whatever Inshallah, Amen,

can work for millennia throw in for luck
at the bargaining table, sipping
endearing wine of long-familiar gestures tasted

on tongues together again.

Shared Consciousness

Under our network of noise,
purred, hissed, murmured whispers
carry breath of living

creatures holding secrets,
who approach listening
hard whether to trust us

with all senses in the open
and make our home their lair,
who come out evenings to roam

the dark hours, and we take in
their likeness moving us
in consciousness we recognize

a light in their eyes we have
stepped into and, moving in
shared consciousness, wanting most

one able to love us best.

The Way

The way kittens are cute,
and cucumbers cuke,

the way young lovers make a new
crew of two,

and sea and sky are seasoned
with blue,

the way clouds, moving museums,
redo portraits, slowly, askew,

the way a squirrel can shoot
between speeding wheels and scoot

through, the way I try
at times to walk in your shoes,

or mornings I let you snooze,
and *No* is not rebuke,

and our diamond is dust
in the court of Hullaballoo,

the way the sun doesn't always
come out, or on cue,

just as Osip Mandelstam's friends
never called him Joe,

the way a lawyer given a chance
will usually sue,

the way a dealer wants all
hands in view,

the way a pitcher picks up
his catcher's least move,

the way a better venue for George W.
would've been Bellevue,

the way summer gardens grow
more than rainbow hues,

and until there's a two-state solution,
or conversion of the Jews,

and the sky at night is not history
in pursuit,

the way passing an open doorway
can revive the eye,

the way from night of winter solstice, I too
champ at the bit for the two,

three precious seconds of sunlight that accrue
each day as our claim on summer comes due,

the way one who praises
peels sour grapes and the dust

when red roses rust, and never loses
hold of the shining tray,

and in winter holds memory of summer
sunlight under the skin all day,

the way when you're into something true
the language will help you,

the way we're older now
than we ever were, and all is new,

call it love, person-to-person provocateur,
and not only with, but through

you I do.

Late Inheritance

Though the long white limestone road
looks like it ends about here, you don't
want to stop its rainbow-curve-end
leaching colors from the Everglades
given back, so many years.

Old rocks the chain gangs pulverized they must
have wished were walls of their prison.
Is there a law in crisis draws a man back
to ancestors whose grimace appalls
with what they had to survive?

Does luck double in my seventy-seventh year,
or trouble? Merciful moment returning
wavers across closed eyes as I nap in a field—
wake, eye level, tongued smell glands, shadow
that woke me, diamondback stares, sniffs, tastes,
lowers, sidling off, does not take me.

Need to Be New

As April's fevered games find
their green fingerings
flowering to hand,

and small bouffant blooms close—
white petals turning plump
clustered blueberries—

on a day that you feel
the need to be new
to yourself

and take a step
opposite to your nature,
fate that felt

inevitable opens on the possible—
more chancy, but
more charitable—

for the long, slow urging
witness,
aging . . .

unlike the man who on reading
about the evil of drinking,
gave up reading.

If it's a sickness we no longer speak
the language of those reconcilable,
on their feet,

it may be the unspoken onset
of our best to stanch
a sweeping tide of deserts

in the making. The beautiful and true
will have their dawn,
due some other day.

The Farther Side of Dread

Now it comes back, that voyage long
ago, landing in African ports,
like going from sleep-sailing

dream afloat, mesmerized
us at sea, to fleshy, fetid reality. Once ashore,
our captain and officers thought us diseased

already. In port bars, in white shirt and tie, half
bristling half choking at their far table,
their rage cheered us; we laughed

as tribal-scarred girls drinking with us
were a twittering
native chorus, barroom burlesque.

Outside, under orange harbor lights,
we staggered in pairs toward shanties
of tin-roofed walls welded into night.

Virile, virginal, all would enjoy
the fruits of famished sex we hauled ashore
without having to plant the tree. Any

such night spent in haste
would be a night's
unpardonable waste.

Sparks flew, sounds of happy clapping,
smell of wood smoke mixed with
human sewage, the free stripping

down to desire's fulfilling near
the source of pleasures,
without shame or fear.

Was it some reflex to threat
back home made us leap to reach
the farther side of dread,

and see night lightening darkest
continent to dawn?—creation's original
cauldron colors, brightening.

Eye-Crowned

In the oasis of interior rest, come
lie with me on a cushion
of quantum foam

in a sea of dark matter becoming
lighter, like the insight of the blind—
not caring if being watched or not

seen at all, or seen with that look
of the Law: implacable, insatiable, silent
as night holding on to the eyes of the blind.

From ballpark, birdcage, balconies, and malls
comes from all sides a thousand-
sided mirror of a thousand-sided sky

blue that never arrives but stays
wound around the crown
of a human's—who knows why?—

happy or sad eye.

Our Deal

Winter light on a doorknob
that will not open
anymore, such a whimpering
song. The loss of loved ones
now only words, hard enough.

Bring thou down more
than dotage in a croaked voice
harping. Too late, too cold for
new parts. And may those girls
only half-divine if not half so
wild as imagined days,

dance their dirges so
delightfully, and not least
for release to lure and lust,
and the tooth of their youth
not infected yet.

The game we love
to play, the foolishness
when the fire is out
of what we talk about . . .

Task done, it falls as from the tap
of a cask red along
the rim, and everything
within runs away with us.

The past does not last without age
prolonging its hour's wrinkled
hide and folds. Such a shame,
a baboon once thought handsome
now quivers and shivers and cannot chew.

This message will not outlast
body and spirit. There will be no funeral.
This is our deal; and it goes
for all.

Weather Front

Here I am in this depressed economy,
a Johnny-come-lately devotee of George W.'s
economic policy: *Spending money.*

Dark moods in currents
move through
like weather fronts

and the world in ever-greater trouble
just when two lovers feel happiness
between them possible;

and their existence loves
the matter they discover
they're made of,

and not the troubles
but the eyes that have seen them
know they too will

go, from desperado-
dark joy, naked Sunset
Beach, Point Loma, San Diego,

when more than a dream granted,
hearts opened to what they did
not know they'd wanted—

or others—to know; like seeing the dead
on intimate speaking terms with the living
in the same dawn world.

I'm not saying this always happens;
I am saying I would like to
be able to say this happens.

As We Were

Face that I see
and search in for the face
I last saw twenty years ago—
skin flush with glowing beauty,
whose cast of lovers rivals
Mina Loy's and Edna Millay's—
is dry, wrinkled, crushed
crepe shrink-wrap in plain
sight what a thief stole
and replaced with what
the grievous old look like
as they feel in their bones
what no one sees, the dull
way we change nightly
in the dark and are
remembered only
as we were.

Older, Knowing the Hazards

Older, knowing the hazards, touching,
going, paying attention to the inward reach

rage provokes in men, granting
the troubles we're heir to, remembering

the world arguably worse as it is, I tried
to imagine the source of the instance

of my end. I tried and failed, and grateful
for the day, turned to chores of the world

where no one goes with no cost from birth,
at what risk, at what loss, the shine in every

perishing spark, every cry in every tongue
crying in the darkest dark, and the small

black angel that morning's tar-winged stain,
outspread at the edge of the road, stays

like lasting dawn.

Alien

When favor pours on all you can't keep
in mind, whatever kind—ragged, unkempt, random—
speak for me, the legend I've come for, under my feet,

others yet uncovered, pleased to live the gift, recall,
received, no more punished for being at all. Say no more
of exile and return. Removal relents, approval

atones, in my own home, in my own bed.
Tell them I can't come, being
exile's poster boy. A cloud

draws near, whoever applauds this work
that's flawed applauds the maw few
can resist. For the names in lights, the quick

bottom-feeders prevail. Raise your praise so
hungered for, and much more. I do not hate the state
I suffer from—and for; this place I walk about, though

alien, I breathe, and look, and see, and more—much more.

Should Tomorrow, as We Know It

Now the miracle near growing
tired of being
lived is breathing

out of a loved one, open
eyes still
shining light within . . .

It is not easy for anything
to give up
shining . . .

And such a family!—
Slippage of the human
roots grown into the tree.

From the young, eyes darting bright—
from the elderly, indrawn,
reflective—light,

we have been granted the greed in flight
between eternities to take
as much as we like

from whomever, to sustain however
costly the wager, war, as the surest
way to profit and endure.

Winter evergreen, ride, abound
with the Prince of Spring Fever
in the Insolvable Inevitable that's bound

this way, touching everything alive,
reaching everywhere, should tomorrow, as we know it,
arrive.

SECTION 2

The Pages of the Calendar

The pages of the calendar are falling fast;
it was always so,
they don't last.

What's new is the mildew
on the sills of heaven,
my mother's sore, arthritic elbows

lean as they used to, three stories above
street traffic—open market, briny mongers, fishy-
smelling, throat-clearing hawkers—now

I see her those afternoons she sat
in all the years that weigh
more now than when she saw she had

no choice in kin, home, husband, but alien
land and language she could refuse, almost
like not being there,

but in cool evenings in the souk
under silken awnings, tapping of
silver-and-goldsmiths, and holding

her mother's hand. Here, she stared from
high above a loud, crowded street in diesel air;
high, but not so high

she could know someday how dreary
a life, daily boredom, comes
to housewife and harem girl.

Each loved one gone changes
our seeing and feeling
the world that leaves us

distant, detached, strangely
indifferent to what one
day would make true.

Meanwhile, in winter, like everyone,
we raise our wan faces anytime
the sun deigns, however faint, to shine

on our faces, like mirrors
in which we wish
to see ourselves appraised.

Etiquette of Defeat

After we kids were born, late
1930s, my father in the fifty years left to him
Did not get laid.

I read it in a letter he wrote
To me but never sent
Before he died at eighty-eight.

Bearing six years of marriage, three kids,
My mother laid down
The law: That's it!

He couldn't tell me while I lived at home.
He was not that kind. He was Old World
Old. Ottoman Empire old. Baghdad-born,

In the end of the 19th century's oil-rigged, colonial-world old.
You did what you were told: by Sultan, Young Turks,
East India Co., Turkish Petroleum Co., Torah-told.

From Baghdad to Brooklyn in the Depression,
Quiet, patient, long-suffering, in his mid-40s,
Acquired a matchmaker, a bride, refugee

For life. For Orthodox wives, divorce was no option;
For men, flight. In our neighborhood, a husband
Would go to work one day and not return.

My father didn't drink, stray, or leave
For fifty years. *"She seemed,"* he wrote,
"Allergic to it, enough

for a lifetime," proving women's power
To say No, no matter a husband's rabbinical duty
To lay with his wife on the Sabbath for an hour.

In moments hauled from the storm
Of late emotions, I try to
Imagine (having never seen) them

Hug, kiss, touch, gaze, hint
Feigned affection, some glimpse
Of shared physical pleasure, a glint

Of unpremeditated joy a boy
Could rouse, belated treasure, however now
I wish them back in time. No way.

Freud was a crock: there was no Oedipal shock, nor
I witness; never saw them fuck; never willed
Anyone killed, but wished him less quiet, less meek, more

Her! But no matter the weather, in suit and tie,
Door-to-door, running errands, stock clerk, salesman, owner
Of his own dry-goods store that didn't last:

"Of all my jobs, dying is my last"... Never owning a car,
A lifelong walker, he meant to leave as little footprint—
Carbon or otherwise—as possible.

And you cocksmen, who crow of the women you've had—
How hungrily they drain your loins and have
Your heaped, backed-up ashes hauled,

Imagine a moment it all
Denied, refused—not deferred: *Verboten!* What'd be
your take on half a century's blue balls?

How'd you do it, Dad? I didn't stick around.
Families are to flee. A coast away, one day
I heard you did get laid, in parted ground.

The Joy in My Father's Surprise

It wasn't often nor was it fluent, the rare
times he'd laugh; his face,
most used to anonymity—stoic, spare,

introverted Baghdadi, hard on his pleasures.
Surprised out of his daily worry
over bills, rent, groceries—a seizure

of shy, childlike laughter flushed
his tired, work-weary face into
relaxing muscles, skin blushed

a smooth, rosy surface
after the first laugh settled. For such
joy to break out, he'd have had to lose

command of himself. Joy that wins by
losing, relieved, at last thrilled to be
surprised, as only long-suffering can be.

Chocolate

Incorrigible teenage boys leaning
on the boardwalk railing, evening
greying the salt-white shore
and the bobbing buoys we'd made for
so manically earlier that day, in the inner
tire tubes we inflated for life preservers . . .
Summer's daydreaming darlings, we
were the heat's beneficiaries,
our sun-burnt buzzing bodies
in our clothes stored like batteries.
Keen to stay put, then keener
in the approaching dark to go farther
toward the sharp light of stars
so blown apart and blinking up there
from which our stare drew back,
as if their winks were points on
a journey in their pulsing way
down here, to the clammy salt-ocean
air we breathed. Though our legs ached
from standing still with no break,
the brown suede shoes we stood in felt
soft as melted chocolate on our feet.

There Is a House, Barely Standing

There is a house, barely standing, only the lost
Can find, within whose beams a nest
Of lives happened, the way cement starts moist,

Then hardens. In the walls, the wood
Held sounds inside their rings,
As old, redbrick tenements did.

Whatever love might
Have made of mixed, mismatched natures,
Time would tease apart,

And soon-to-be desolation,
Lapping there, loves to lull,
Lingering like a lesion.

Cell calling to cell
Quiet as snow crystals falling
On a bell rung for the evening meal;

Cell from cell, fallen lids
From eyes, and nowhere
Abide

Those once warm bone and gristle,
Pounded in a pestle, ground
For retrieval,

Who rest a moment back when
Happiness rushed up, then away,
With us on the Sea Beach Line to Coney Island,

Light and space on the horizon's
Curved distance made summer
Swell. Reachable. Strewn.

Wonder-Wanting

Wonder-wanting angels on the fence still
working to make sense, by the time
we come to our senses will we,

if not beaten senseless, radiate
late in our later days' century's
silver light

on a shell, like a snail
building a soul slowly
following a funeral?

Take it, break it naked
before it costs more
scant time, and make

enough loving
to give the dead
a taste of living,

and on familiar terms, exchange
greetings, woken
in the same dawn, on the same beach,

while sorrowing—strung
on the tireless wide wings tipped
with last things—

goes the way a bulb is lost in sunlight, or black
as a Cadillac falling
like a meteor dissolving in the dark.

Young Reader

Turning his face, turning pages,
descending to where deep
body engages, already fading,
looking up from the book he
flows into, eyes grasp and
hunger on, following
what won't let go,
and if a moment he'd pause,
a ray of reality would be
freed as applause.

Birthday

The eighty candles on the cake
My eighty years would brightly make,
Unlit instead, mark the season's dark

In which I do not—and never did—celebrate
The arc of decades they would orchestrate.
As my mother, asked for her birth date

Said, *Doomsday! Why commemorate*
Bad luck
With a date!

Desire, desire, desire,
Lacking only
The mechanism that's required.

Instead, for February's coldest, shriven, stingy sake,
I blow on cinders that jump the crack
To break out, before light and lark, a little spark.

He Was Changing

He was changing; not to be
Traced back and parceled to origins.
He was not there. He

Would not go through that unraveling
From the primal petri dish
At the beginning;

Shade of a shade,
Keeping an appointment
He never made.

He was listening from the edge of a place
Where the inner ear hears what goes
Unspoken in a face.

He listened for the unspoken
Bid or need or hidden deed
For what it might betoken,

Like a new sensation, an open
Window he had not thought there
Even to look out from.

A time came, in order to live,
He could no longer afford
To inhabit the negative.

He'd leave it to the ancient runner
With the day's stolen glass eye
That won't shut, who appears

At watering holes of fading herds,
And those under ash that once
Covered the land, never heard

From again. Steam, steel, picks, rails, rescind
The wolf packs playing with fire's heat—
Waves blowing in on gusts of wind,

And the sea, nodding in its salt,
Whose hiss had lost
None of its vault.

What the Sky Collects

When evening rolls out stars on sea and sand,
remind yourself, alone with this, you are
not unique, though still alone,

and not what matters. Sky
collects memories of our days;
they must reach the stars by

now. When you gather your pain
like loose change that comes
and goes to gain

the sympathy of others who also gather
their pain and wait, like you, alone,
though not unique and not what matters,

what's been said, and still more
what's done and not done, called
and recalled, compressed into carbon, scatters.

Odysseus, Older

1.

As when a gun fires and the sound scatters,
Making connections with forces
That occur later,

My life is not as it was in the old days;
I have no name for long ago, beating
Tides and racing hull-biting waves

To bring me to a life I'd enter
My dotage tomb in a bald light
Of a morgue that each dawn, disinterred,

Comes to die in yesterday's underwear.
In this close, contagious sky wrapped
Over the land like insulation that covers

The blue, and in so black a zodiac, I see
In faces growing heavier, their aged
Grief in a moment's fatigue that filled me

Once with pity for human frailty, now in sight
Of their fall, a steady stream, nagging,
Tendering survival, like a kept-secret

Insight of the blind, or how women instinctively sense
Trouble brewing, or about to, and widen
Their margin of safety, increasing distance.

2.

Back then, the sea was a cradle of days
With no mirror, leaves with no veins,
Mornings with no sun, birds with no cries,

Of humans no scent, of bones no cradle
Not a jungle of jaws, and of the sea
Each trough a wrinkled

Trench to drop into. I would rather sundown's long magic
Carpet of light's lowering hour, when grass goes
To dark coppery green almost black, back

To what daylight delivers, pleasure
In tomorrow recovered, replayed,
Varied, tinted anew for good measure.

Moles are digging
Deeper, squirrels chewing faster, better
At begging,

And the spread evergreen screens
To slivers and glints
A sky-wide band that gleams

Sundown's glowing orange
Beam deepening through foliage, unrolling
Red as a soaking bandage.

Least Bittern

In old age, when smallest actions
take most effort in the crash
economy of elder mobility,

how soon talk becomes thistles
in the throat; each citizen, Least
Bittern: small, camouflaged, hidden,

straddling reeds, kept thin,
feeding in depths too deep
for other herons, and alarmed, freezes

open-mouthed for savoring
danger on the air, swaying in place like
marsh reed to predators, swaying.

So do we crave such a kind
of phantom antenna as
the insight we imagine for the blind,

which takes them further in feeling: heard hint
stitched to felt hunch, scent as indrawn
touch, stench of the hutch, matter's

rich rottenness—which would send our senses
reeling from such quick-shifting cues.
Each night, sleep brings

daylight bodies sinking back
to an unlived life, submerged, springing
from as far away as ground calling

for change in heart, home to change, that's always
surprise, and arrived, will go
unrecognized at home, calling in smallest, stillest, farthest

whistle.

SECTION 3

The Curve

The cats are in: out of seven,
four remain; at each count,
there are fewer of them

as winter comes near
to throwing overboard hearts and heaves
and hungers on like the hunger

that feeds the heaven of virgins
unveiled, available, and loves to pieces
their promised, piecemeal martyrs; or as when

in an animal's eyes we're seen,
held in a grip tighter than a gaze,
guarded, still, curious, then

assured, easing until unthreatened,
losing interest in our presence,
we've been released, just when

fixed on us before turning aside,
like the barely remembered summer gone by,
drawn back to the bottomless well running dry.

As one gets older and slips into seeing less
in the human world of the best
of what there is,

grief
cuts eloquence
brief.

So, bless the voices stressed
leaving cell phone messages, one hand on wheel
in freeway traffic, wishing Merry Christmas,

who, distracted, will, statistically, die
in holiday traffic which, honest, is more a mob
on wheels, for we're not able to tell

what's real when we come to the hedge
we peel off and go floating
over, feeling a dreamy uncertainty on the edge

of which world we're in, like a story that leaves
out a too-real page
unturned in our lives

we look forward to and find later
not treasure in the flowering
but the remembering after, and once more

I know I'll be slow behind the curve
when absolute zero unpacks its bags and installs April's
sunny tunes and smiles on walls we fasten to live on earth.

Lunch

Before any recent world events I could stand
to tell, come the storms
I can't.

If our issue is headlines prying wide-
opening vistas of more
speakable horror, imaginable dread,

soon our issue
will not be worth the toilet
tissue it's issued

on. How pretend
to core scruples in a country
held at gunpoint and couldn't

care less: children first
gone in a flash, the light of their future
dawn spent in a shellburst;

or a mother's thousand-yard stare off a cliff,
with no cranny or nook
of human comfort left.

Men go to war to mingle
with other men they find and mangle
in the news they fill.

War's big winner—
media—is everywhere
sought after,

subscribed, cherished, quoted, with barely time
to sell new details of disaster before old ones
arrive, packed, like in-laws you'll have

to survive. Even stars, for the sake of longevity,
spend, like us, their entire lifetime
resisting collapse in gravity,

otherwise in a big crunch's
gorgeous exploding disarray, the display
of nova-glowing innards is other galaxies' lunch;

or the delicate Asbergian walnut-nut—
who, when he breaks one, feels the pain
on behalf of the nut.

No use to sit and wait
in hope; so sit close
to the exit

door, where December, disarmed,
(God willing!), draws close dawn's spring-
clearing wide horizon.

On the Menu

Eager as an heiress in a hurry
to be widowed and—not remarry—re-
merry,

I wish it could be a lovelier thing
to wait out winter
for return of spring,

that taste in the mouth tasting
sweet mouths and better days
in their passing;

the garden's bare grays, dun greens
dying back, ghost-
furze darkening overgrown

moss, and stone bringing
what my face will look like
before spring. There's a taste to living

before leaving, like a new climate to seasons
that catches the tail of our habits and calls
them out, annulling their reasons.

Being against injustice is like being against death,
wrote Fernando Pessoa, with that much chance,
for what it's worth.

Asked about his Thanksgiving, a friend offers
"Normal is not
on the menu anymore."

What Gamblers Know

Through needled sleeves of winter evergreen,
blood-orange sundown more deeply
staining the later hours, leaving the scene,

things that slip away—smells, cities, friends—have come
to please you who've come
as always in troubled times

to stay. Families scattered, houses lost, jobs kaput, light
going out in the world we know is the new
we navigate from inside

roles we choose, no clue
from which anyone has returned
to tell you

how much closer to the speed
of light hope has to travel to keep
from being annulled by the law of fortune

turning bad. Gamblers know,
no fortune loves you, though it tells
you so,

like the warm, nursing bodies whose tissues
once made milk
for sons who,

sent to war, are
given the bravest songs;
mothers who condone sacrifice

of other mothers' sons, and fathers
whose jobs talk other fathers
to offer up their kin, are ours.

Bird, Are You Still

As living tends to be more alive
on the wing, or else quicker
speared than allows a sigh

for news of distant deaths and near
capital, collateral, and close-
up damage, I wonder,

Bird, are you still
on the wing, and your song,
wish's wormhole

to warmer portals, so keen
a sound, makes a mood almost
making up what can't be seen

or felt yet? Somewhere
is summer,
and you there,

are you still foraging
to us, you promissory, necessary,
startling thing?

SECTION 4

Cannot Contain

Ghost-light stars, steaming loam,
dawn smelling of rock in air
we can't see but manage to climb;

leaves that unfold in their own
code, lives coiled in
their own brain-folds strewn

into the light the white
elevator morning climbs,
crowns, and the leaves start

building cells from light
streaming down, growing
instructions to break out.

Sensation

Keeping count of loss and less
Than gain, against the grain, the grain
All knots, new hewn, at cost,

Amourous as addiction almost
Makes up for generations mounted
On their toppled headstones' rest.

Don't scant the scathing tongue. Drink
Until sober; be still and scatter.
Is to be in a better place to think

No place again will
Be as now, and never as good as
Not at all?

Send to school the eyelids that lift
At the rules
We lived,

And now to see their
Feet sink like prey
They'd hunted for,

Sensation springs
Wild, sweet after so long
Strictly sane.

Morning on the Meadow

Glow so near
To all we do and know,
Did you wish we here

Would think of you, light so far
Which has us live
Not as we might, but as our stars—

Extinguished long ago—exert
Present space to actioned feelings
Seen and lived in, quick as a moment

Goes and comes, the dead given
New life through
Our remembering them

As we clean out the old darkness
And scour old smells out of
The inherited house as it collapses,

And for those who lived
On swallowing
Their disgust, who fell

On their knees and fell on a bed,
The dust up ahead
Would be all of their bread,

And only the dew spreading
Morning on the meadow
Could call itself new.

On Track

On such a night when sound betrays
a sleepless flight
of phrase on phrase,

no hushed prayer, but a lifetime's long
express ride makes my song
meaningless, its wrack somehow wrong.

I look outside, the landscape sliding past,
cities, people, the train itself
not meant to last.

When air and eyesight fail, it's clear,
on track, the next
destination near. Sure,

pain isn't personal;
if you don't have it,
somebody else will.

But inside a bit of dirt and dust,
a mighty mash-up of moods
can't help but hoot with disgust.

We'll need to be more than
rainbows in the ranks of fish
to survive the coming rains;

need to be swifter than bats
out of hell hissing bits
of thirst in coming drought.

Singing, Squawking, the Same Music

Dawn gull-squawk and birdsong fly
leaving behind a little
after-flurry of what's gone
of everything that goes. I

watch the trees, their immensities
of age, broken hides, cracked wooden
armor warding off gravity, holding
still, poised, a-sway where they meant

not to stop but simply go
on with today's coming
to find a way in the melee
where governance pales in princely

indifference, and in the forest,
the deep stillness
in the straightness
of the pines, and through

some trick recall bringing their trilling
back, I hear them singing, shrill,
in the same music, as if
they hadn't stopped at all.

Silence Comes That Had Left the Air

Silence comes that had left the air; presence
without sound, even of those above us who fly—
gull, wren, hawk—and fall

like us who walk under new buds
that stud the branches of young apple trees
like belts of bullets.

               What has kept this world
as it is, as we have made and maimed it, must be
dwelling among us, working hard to continue.

No other works harder, none farthest from rest
but roves, none more restless, relentless than
when green comes out of absence; green's breathing

we inhabit; finch and hummer, seed in the leaves—
what desire other than our own makes.

Silence, larger than the tallest tree.

Open Season

Here comes another open season
for jellied jargon smeared as vision—
new dawn, old reasons.

When borders get porous,
count on people
getting nervous,

like a surge of volts
running through a crowded room, the jolt
when famous people meet.

Fame and money's miracle
make all cures
possible, negotiable.

Everyone
here is anyone's
name.

Meet them at the door; bow,
invite them in; come close and
be bowed to.

Let old mouths twist
something still human
from not-yet dust,

and the young use their looks like honey
for as long as they can
get by on funny money . . .

Age is the root that rises
to greet however late the rain,
wherever its kisses.

SECTION 5

Wilder Matter

Words are not reliable,
and those who speak them,
not liable

to keep them. We say
speaking is a way of meaning,
as sand is the countless ways

of crumbling while shifting,
and water a way of being
free while heaving.

Dunes blow away and their waves
realign; the ocean, though, is
another, wilder matter.

Empty Nest

With eyes barely
brushing what's left to see—
solids watery,
water hazy—

outside the window
hangs the empty nest
doves abandoned without
the whistlings their wings

make taking flight,
whose four forlorn notes—
ohoo-hoo-hoo-hoo—at evening
still sound a mating call

we call "mourning."
Far from here, an empire
baptizes with bullets
hearts beating sore

as their feet in the loam
where all noble vows vie
with their larval undertow—
spawned carbon and peptide,

spirochete and capillary—
like the lava-slow dinosaur
fleeing a comet—are we
ever!

This Enterprise

When in summer we go indoors,
and the sunlight we've taken in
endures

awhile, like housefronts that stand,
open-faced, at the long lowering rays
braided with day's perils and pleasures bound

in a golden eye not yet shut, that
lingers on the horizon's eye liner, then closes,
as the sea lulls it to sleep in its salt—

what flashes to follow more
now that shadows lean closer,
and not so strange anymore?

As nothing feels tame on the outer edge,
nothing tame holds
on with age,

when signals emit
hungers stirred
from neglect,

and the wire of listening leads
to picking up secrets no longer
of any value to hide,

or the unexpected kind
of sudden happiness
that lights a new kind of mind

in this enterprise of sighs
that makes it brave
to be alive,

for the happy turn when those who are blessed—
unknowing themselves, unknown
to us—bless.

The Way Trees Grow at Night

Early June 2013, my ignorance refreshes
itself: new season, so why does happiness
so unexpected still taste of bitterness,

and song the grief-tree's fruit itself?
Things stir as in their first hours
of origin and the first birds speed

to their reward, unbarred airborne shooting
stars or rats with wings, here's to the stream's
wealth one dime at a time accruing

loss like the tremor in a bettor's hand,
the sublime running out of steam
like a stream in drought where heaven's

entire musical scale can fit into a wish—
one beat, one note, into the shell of
my paycheck for the joy of watching it vanish.

Along with the repopulation of bees,
I want those bees that coated Pindar's lips
as a boy asleep, with honey,

invisibly out of the light, the way trees grow at night.

What Surviving Is For

As any morning in the shower,
feeling the big
quake near,

when each one prays
it not shake just now, or
we'll be out on our asses . . .

Still, such cherry-
picking
from calamity!

In Ebola land, a doctor
wouldn't barter for his heart
any harder,

the infectious door
cannot narrow
more; and more

than skeletons
in our closets—
worms,

shrunk like the baby spider
back into its corner
from my aimed puff of air.

Sweetness long gone
that came
with the honeycomb,

and fire season
now year-
round,

we enter a season
in which it will not be easy
to hold onto reason,

feeling our body a grounding
for intentions hidden
from ourselves, only knowing

as much as we can afford
living a life in accord
with what surviving is for.

Summer Days More Quickly Falling

Summer days more quickly falling
from the calendar, still-green
pears off the tree.

The sun goes down on a day few birds
bid goodbye, and on islands across
great distances where human whistling once

equaled the birds', no more sweet water-
melon chunks fallen off a truck, prolonging
the ruby edge into summer nightfall.

To have had the birds hear your song
and shift their throats was like laughter
at the laugh that laughs at the last

loose threads that cling, so
say those who know of the elder born
at the source of the Orinoco,

who walks at the head of the herd, first
heartbeat, original footfalls' echo.

Birth Took the Bait

In the sobering-long view
of distance that looks all
the way through,

I'm gone the way a flare leaps
and fuels the day; a nerve ignites
and fuels a pulse that keeps

me stretched, and fades
to what will become of me,
as if a butterfly were made

to fold its wings and re-enter the dead
woven chrysalis
it once shed.

Beaks of birds who earthward break
their songs, in drought soar
to clouds for a drink,

a sip of what earth doesn't offer
anymore, and summer vanishes,
like a stain that was once a shore.

I try to step, leap, fly out of the calendar's ending.
In me, what began is near
done. The links I found, I'm adding

to; links—bits themselves—in a broken
chain. Birth took the bait;
fragments and fibers I'm floating on.

In our sinking,
earthward heading,
is our singing.

Nasty Weather

With mid-October leaf fall comes the swirl
just when you feel you've lived
long enough to be still . . .

Will there be enough sunlit days to ripen
the green cherry tomatoes, little
orphans left on the vine?

Sun rays like slant gold bars, first
trace of chill in the air, wind
picking up, feelers of frost-

bite flaying at the near edge
of impending weather front's
flood, hurricane, landslide's approach.

The nation prepares its memory pools
to soak in, schooled in patriotic puddles
while politicians and their bankers grow

more slick more despicably flagrant
than what's decently wicked, divesting
the weak while a punishing economy

withers on the stalk. Even the face in laughter
dancing in place, overcome
by knowledge of unravelings

to come, begins a happy day
in the midst of dread
days that don't go away,

and the rich, who own the Stock Exchange
allow the rest to keep
their loose, let-fallen change.

At dawn, not aiming at reward,
a warbler leaves the branch, a flutter
of what's gone, of everything that is going.

October

October, pennant weather, where time goes
in the outfield to die. Here's a branch bobbing,
just alighted from; buzzing, humming—

bird wings too swift to spot. Leaf to leaf,
sunlight shimmers on a fiber-optic net,
the garden a glisten of slipping glimpses.

On a silken film in space, faces
recently dead unspool, each
a spilled star in my direction

until a flashing glance sees
me through; a galaxy
of sand grains in the eye of a camel

without water by the god of nomads
who raises the sun more
easily than water in a well; dog-

in-reverse, biting believers, unbelievers,
who bite each other. But you're here.
You came here. You walk these streets. You allow

things to happen. You open the door. You
inhale air. Far past the day
you thought you'd end at long ago,

evening inches over ancient
pyramid night in this
time of year wolves blow

shofar howls, eyes so fixed
on prey cross in unifocal grip,
scalpel-sharp as sunlight after surgery . . .

How little will remain, and how heavy
the weight of that telomere tail
shrinking, as the cell is extinguished.

Mandelstam, exiled in Voronezh, so starved
for readers, recites his poetry over the telephone
To his NKVD surveillance agent;

Frozen days floating, the last feather
Turned gray, not as though he'd seen a ghost, but as though
Born a ghost, lasting no longer than good-bye.

November

Wind-driven rains on the raw
plank boards blacken the garden fence
and sweep the halved, gnawed
walnut shells squirrels drop for a chance

at later. On the lemon tree, late
ripening in leafy clusters:
green galaxy, yellowing suns.
Miniworlds in this world

the sailor song begun
in youth recoiling now
in age unforeseen: pared
down, earthbound, driven

body wizened as by a wizard with claws.
Of late, his gaze withdraws, a kind
of second childhood, this time orphaned,
while in the eyes of the young he sees—

as they see—himself here, now.
Or would there be instantaneous
new knowledge, precise propelled
blows so quick, so knit into flowing

perpetual motion to make solids
thaw, and in the waves between blinks holding still
the weight of a raindrop on an eyelid trying
to open as here and now

arrives and, as today, would
deliver always.

For Allan Kornblum

This day after your death, one day
Before Thanksgiving (I have a bone
To pick!), the way sundown's long, low
Lit beams make cathedrals of the trees, makes furry
Caterpillars of waving cattails.

While the world goes on the same outside, I recall
You in the doleful Iowa cold, stamping your feet,
Hawking your first Toothpaste mimeos on street corners
For a quarter to buy a burger for dinner.

Winter coming on, no less cold for global warming,
Survival equals arrival, and deepening our descent
In a moment's duration, deepens feeling's human depth.
But everything is the same for you. Spreading out,
Reddening twilight with a single death concentrates
The mind on the sensory synapse of one who once lived

And is no more, whose face flits on
And on, not yet gone but about to, distant human
Hum already receding, unfinished trace
Of living that no longer is the case,
Makes us stop and feel the rush going out
Of all the years at once, and takes us with it.

SECTION 6

I See the Urge to Care in the Current Carnage

I see the urge to care in the current carnage
carries you
                    toward wreckage.

I see the despot who wants you to say nothing
after hearing his words, whether you find them
freeing or frightening,

wants you to know wherever you go from here
is laced, spiked, timed
to go off later,

I see with so much more space around
than bargained for now
housing much more sadness,

and a branch of night thickens
and makes solid
geology under the skin.

Nothing here is not lost:
I see to go on is going
out at all costs.

Listen Up!

When leaders speak of pinpoint operations,
The people know to abandon their homes.

When generals talk of limited targets,
The people know to get out of town.

When ministers talk of surgical strikes,
Doctors know to evacuate the hospitals.

When statesmen talk of ceasefire,
The people know to flee.

When a foreign power prepares war games,
People get ready for invasion.

When the president speaks to buoy up the people,
Get ready to go down fast.

Bleeder

Don't bother him with news
That's no news: the best and brightest kill,
The wicked are worse.

He's got a nose-
Bleed redder than
A Nolde poppy to nurse.

It's gushing faster, redder, rarer than blood
In Gaza, that fetid open-air prison, less
Fish in a barrel than guppies in a cup.

The rabbis egging Bibi on are drinking
It up, rabid as soccer fans for their coveted
Cup. What's up with this clown whose yanking

Is so biblically in lock-step death would rather wait
Than shake him. Now look!—no dice!—stained big
As a billboard, red as a toreador's cape—no escape.

Bibi, the shotgun at the wedding, mugs
Obama on his home turf. Oh, shut up!
Mercy, mercy . . . *a glück af dein kop*.

I Played Alone. I Was the King

I played alone. I was the king
of central power behind
trades and never having

to fight civil war since I counted
enforcing laws I added to the books
as countering the added enemy living among

my subjects in a city built from
miracles of mortar,
brick and stone,

where sunlight smelts
gold the sparrows fight for
in noonday melt,

and under chestnut trees, summer's chiffon
women, in silence, sinning; men far off
at war, winning.

I was revered
beyond reason, except for the jobless
rioters, prisoners, poets, profiteers.

All those behind desks
who know about smoothing
mistakes, and never listen when you ask

for advice in legal matters, knew,
and smiled, as if to say, believe the world
as declared forbidden, and stay

the ruler of the secret you
alone are to be
the rest of your days.

Another Religion

From ice to water to steam,
the way chemical conversion
is another religion,

mystery unspoken,
but there, visible, working
in our midst, a pinecone

cathedral in the needle
grass scabbed with mud, and spins
toward the gnarly, nearly invisible,

which needs no passport there.
Whatever signs and marvels can
be made seen, even more

than seeing is believing, believing sees
more than seeing
believes, like a fixed gaze

on some distant place or scene, a stare
growing out of what is
not there, regained, or

the way chemical conversion
from ice to water to steam is
another religion's resurrection,

what we hanker for,
to be startled again,
before perishing like a prayer.

A Blow Not Yet Felt

From the yard with unbarred gates, a bird
stirs, as if for first flight,
and speeds to its reward,

and old, hard, cold
regret rushes in to spill, in a drop,
its hot mother lode winced at today

even more than the Law
on the books would fulfill,
and had you served the time,

you would have been out by now,
though running out of steam,
out of time to see human endeavor

dedicated to mass human
and animal slaughter's tidal sway.
After the fewer doings with humans

here's a new raw breed to better know,
and closer share with, in the weeds.
Otherwise, living in fear of a blow

not yet felt, out of sight,
is grounds for fright. As voices
wrested from captives are not their choice,

their captors' voices pollute the air
with rehashed verbiage that at the moment
spoken is already garbage:

news of the lost, found;
the lost who have found a way
to flight and hit a steel wall

risen out of the earth—that fells them.

Horses

Catwalk beauties think
they can bat away
time with slow winks,

slinking down the runway.
Time never keeps its word, or keeps
appointments it never made. I

concur, and wish a wind, calling,
watching, slowly
falling

wide, waits, mute, as glowing
light dissolves
into a flowing

of desert people licked
by molten liquid
sunlight, lucky to have picked

sturdy horses able to stand for long
without using muscle power: skeleton
and spinal column, a self-supporting

structure. If suddenly surprised
by an image outside their gaze, alarmed,
whinnying, they shake their head to readjust

their vision, sounding the alarm,
and the foals are herded for safety
in the center of the swarm.

The Blue of You

Not a wing of hawk in the sky,
not a crumb of cloud,
not a clue

in the blue of you,
seasoning sky
with salt of sea winds

driven through, where once
water rested
like Buddha

evaporating, not a wing
in the sky, not a crumb,
for even the smallest

fisted hand of the shrunken
living trunk
hunger just felled.

Renew the Low Stream

Renew the low stream with
singing,
renew the slow stream with
falling
water, hear it new,
slaking thirsts
of desert people
licking sun's molten
liquid light.

Let alone night, no history
is as blissed, cursed,
rending, raking
ashes, worse,

        to renew the weary
      stream laughter loves
to shower a man licking himself clean
of the residue of guns.

We have taken ourselves
out of compassion
for earth's creatures, as if we
will never have to suffer
its need ourselves,

lowly stream in the land,
lowest of
waters in the earth,
lowest
flowing, gathering cold deep dark
up, out-
spreading sunrise.

A Loaded Gun

In a time made small
by the hunger of the hungry,
the fullness of the full,

with events taking their course
hidden behind the language
served up to us,

to its republic of shoppers, America tells
"What you want,
consume it all!"

"If you want to become invisible,
become poor," Simone Weil
wrote in her journal.

Even the rare good man as leader cannot think
craftily enough to avert
greed and treachery in his ranks,

as outrage of the weak and destitute
is snuffed, and decimation of black youth
expands to critical mass, the hopeless

are harried by an idea
carrying them like a river
they've been promised to be carried by:

that they be consulted, recognized,
cared for, fed, consoled,
eased, protected . . .

For the dispossessed to read,
must first open the blank
book of bread

before debt forgiven
is death marked down,
if not withdrawn.

In America, failure's a kind of death. No rest or
contemplation allowed. Pitilessness of the rules
we live under, and death a kind of failure.

No vote will end or mend
this, nor a poor man at night,
like a rich man, be attended

on scavenger streets
owned by politicians who own
the police who own the bullets,

and the Law, like a loaded gun,
melting at night, fading away, steals
back at dawn, still a long way from

coming clean. What a coming
dawn that would be, instead of
a gathering in the air for a plummeting!

At the checkpoints of last entry, pity
those who await judgment
when the old women have their say

who have picked at the old stones of the past
and the present leaves only a few
minds sane, and not the best.

*"Courtesy is the key
to safety,"* reads my ribbon of Chinese
fortune cookie,

and the messenger of promise,
delivering losses, keeps
in touch, lips pursed, if not a kiss.

SECTION 7

Petals in the Rose

The rose of dawn that separates darkness
And distance into shapes and colors returning
In the mirrors of morning;

The rose of sunrise that branches
Into many vines;

The rose of science that probes
New theories, deeper dimensions;

The rose of religion that enshrines
The past and keeps it
                            coming;

The rose of absence, more
Consuming
Than presence;

The rose of one
In a conversation who prefers
Silence;

The rose of falling
Under the feathery
Fingers of flattery;

The rose of hands and feet
In place
Of a vanished tail;

The rose on the scale of the one
With most to hide
Who acts freest;

The rose of history that rots
The vine it grows on;

All await petals in the rose of the future, so
Imminent already
Swallowing the present.

What the Dead Do

Now the lure of a lit matchstick face
Flares, fans out,
A loved one's smile lost

Not long ago, his hand on the wheel
Of hidden facts, and mouthing scathing
Bites of the Zionist right, he'd taken on the gall

To displease everyone easily pleased, to disarrange
The inherited hierarchies. He wanted the intense
Feel of swift, bold change,

That the light in his time
Be as fiercely bright
As the light filling him,

Whom to address as *you* creates
The fiction of a life
Still approachable, afloat.

Having chosen to resist,
Let him rest. Let him
Do what the dead do best.

For Steve Kowit

> *As this comes in*
> *Call you*

I call you
The apples are red again in Chandler's Valley,
redder for what happened there, remembering
Steve & me reading Patchen over and over, held
in that round, ripened sadness that binary
sound made out of what was not said; mystery
we came back to feel the undercurrent
running through . . .

        Was it that we felt the line between
living and non-living growing thin, like now? absence
that weights, echo that ripens?

        When a loved one dies,
the world feels different, distant, detached, alien,
and people more intimate, visibly burdened, feeling
what it feels like to begin forgetting the world
we live more adrift in.

Now all the words you won't get to say, I'll miss . . .
That'd be one way to begin—bogus!
There won't be any:
You said all you had to in any single poem: utter,
unmistakable clarity over which future PhDs (you'll get
a kick out of this!) will grind their teeth, cheated
of obscure, scholarly allusions, like body
parts there'll be no need to autopsy. Perverse, heartless,
that in the moments you were dying, the flowers
outside still had hours.

Even to say you're dead refutes itself
like an oxymoron; so alive, still yammering, arguing,
provoking, protesting, agitating, advocating,
        lost in the bright air
Of impossible gaiety, incomparable youth, passion
And blather, that feast made of fine talk . . .

And something you were saying to me:
"We are a failed species"... this from a poet protesting
for justice for the weak and dispossessed forsaken
into havoc, which that committee of one, Fernando
Pessoa, said, is like protesting death.

No matter, you were in the mix, passionate pessimist,
so attentive, curious, bemused, compassionately
hip to the cry that humor hides—and amorous
as addiction—our crazed self-regard and self-deceit;
you confessed yours, shedding light
in which to admit our own.

Late teen, slender, nimble tennis pro,
in midlife, vegetarian, putting on weight as if
compassion's caloric intake increases with knowledge
of personal grief, communal guilt for the suffering
our living inflicts on others: unhooked, removed,
undressed, flogged, fucked, spilled, dissolved, disappeared
down the chute, terrorized as penned, prodded cattle
nose-kiss, knowing they're on the way to slaughter,
and the truth of Singer's clinching line you'd repeat,
Each day is Treblinka for the animals, still makes me queasy.

And no advantage in the knowledge that there is more
to know, like prey made more alive for being hunted.
Then, look back on those long-ago, oblivious
days we call nostalgia?—*nostos,* the return home:
some vision the past had given and taken back;
some compassion we allow ourself, as to a stranger.

It's the old days, knocking at the door, asking
Can we stay?... Memory, meant to be safe in; what
we know and love, better than what we don't know ...

And when did remembrance become
our future?—*feast made of fine talk,*
we so excitedly partook, perhaps mistaking mania
for meaning we would ride like musicians
in the middle of their music, aware of the magic
going down; great, like the ultimate party
you don't remember.

Once, on acid, you had a vision: posed, scout
on horseback, frozen fresco, bugle to your lips
about to blow . . . and you did, all along, blowing
your delicious, barbed denunciations of power
with such gleeful, cackling, irrefutable gusto much
like Nietzsche's *optimism of a desperado.*

In the light of this midday June, we watch legions
of the living reach up for the wrinkled shirt of dawn
soon to be bloodied, piling like all lives that have sought
sunrise while under midnight's star, and envy
the stones' hardness we inhabit just to not be
for a moment. Now that you're gone, so much
space opens to house so much more sadness.
Who will there be to cut the cake at the feast
and sit down with and eat the actual
lived "Mysteries," of which you made
legend of our youth?

Call you, I call you,
And if I know you, no matter how many tributes, elegies, blurbs
are made for you, too honest to be taken in by myths made
of you after you leave, you'd be sorely anxious, frenetic
in fact, as in life, for those left behind, as each loved one's
absence strikes and binds and knots connective cords tighter,
deepening ties, with the life taken.

Before There Can Be No More

Before there can be no more
Of what there is, might there be
Nothing more? No door

There anymore?
Not closed—
No longer . . .

Like a border
Barrier brick—
Walled over?

Sure, there is the cost,
There is
The dust

We believe cast
Like valuables by those
Who were lost. Lest

The urge
To care carry you
Toward wreckage,

May this, then, bearer
For how long of current
Pulse, a while longer share

In the live, particular pressures
Making ripe disturbance, clueless
Confusion of us, pulse

On the cold
Gripping wind's stone door—
Step, and air open on the rutted roads.

Out of a Depth, Motiveless, Bare

1.
New dawn arriving like a will
rich enough to reveal its blond
bounty and beautiful spill,

a day to fully live,
no longer dredging the habit
of inhabiting the negative ...

But first, the nagging woe
when you are about to learn
something you don't want to know,

which strikes repeated, repentant bolts
through blurred motives, masked
intentions seeming their opposites,

and the need to believe
all means justify the righteous
ends, like the self-deceived;

and the daily ganging-up of body
parts breaking down, like any
chance at the lottery.

And there was something going on
in the current of language, like a home
in the clouds that keeps changing form,

a feeling of disappearing he will have
when writing, for one could
not be anonymous enough.

Today, walking up the street, behold!—
in sunlight, feeling fully here and
a citizen of the world.

2.

Today there was no unspoken
bid or need or hidden deed he'd have
to listen to for the ill it might betoken.

At times, he can clearly hear
the truth in how naked a voice sounds,
out of a depth motiveless, bare.

And now the bearing of breath is not his
alone anymore, but one of the mass
on earth which had grown tired of his

touchiness to slights, of intelligence
so peevish it left no hope
but a counterspike in vengeance

for this enterprise of sighs
that makes one brave
in being alive.

3.

Not absentminded, but most
presentminded
of the past,

the elderly—obsessed with measure
and movement, timing dosage, dimming
appetite, ebbing desire—

lose the struggle when broken
of caring, and left with barely
a self for the last humiliations,

while the hyped, hormonal young
rock with rolling spit-lubed
studs in lips, nose, tongue.

Now he knows what awaits
him, like everyone:
the common, uncaring fate,

or was the light he was looking for,
which he'd wanted to see and be seen in,
too wan to care, too bright to bear? Or,

virtues unmasked, could he live—
and revel in his irrelevance? All
or nothing. Take or leave.

Answered Prayers

I don't believe God exists,
though I sometimes wish He did: imagine the blame
we could heap: for the child fallen into a pit; for the next

bullet the poor will have to eat; for botched cures,
colds, cancer; for our crooked Congress's
outstretched hands; for those unaware

of the land mine underfoot; for those who piss
on their victims' pleas. Let Him take
the rap for war, floods, drought, the usual evils. This

Cosmic Fair Play—exact
as perfect pitch—what God would want
or grant such creaturely liberties? Imagine that!—

a glinting irritant in God's eye
whose celestial blue-tinted
cornea composes the whole sky's

horizon, nearly inviting intimacy.
Sunset's temple in lush living pulmonary
spectacle, a show of divinity's

powers from pastel to astral solar palette
every evening, and never the same
show twice. What an act!—

like a painter for whom the amount of paint
splashed on work clothes shows
seriousness of intent,

whose worth is granted—in hunger's
delirium all near spent—the full
stock of Eden's answering prayers.

My Book That Came by Way of Woe

My book that came by way of woe
will go the way that I will go, poorly
wrought, next-to-last thought, nowhere to

send this hopeless mission unless with more
conviction, off to the city for retribution,
for a look less somber, less sore, more

fun. Work, flawed, that draws
applause, adds to the list of praise to resist,
though hungered for.

This atmosphere craves the diamond rings
the beginning's outer rim, origin's
atomized carbon dust, is circling.

Here, my feet have not yet felt the favor
of enough metrical feats I have come
and stay for. I relent shedding the tears

I atoned with. Perish the thought. If God will
prefer blasphemy, let us kiss the soul carnally.
If my book were a look, it could kill.

Pressed

Mildew on the sills of heaven,
years weigh more now
than earlier times given

to see gifts given today
erased in the fading
light of a later day, or find a way

to trace through space and find in time,
how a wish, a curse, to take effect, first
moves into unforeseeable sight lines;

or carried like a kiss on the lips pressed
deeper into existence in a cry from
so far back it almost gathers up what is lost.

Abyss all around presses
so close on
the peaks, so close . . .

while walking in full sunshine,
no hitches, feeling as healthy as a well-
lubricated machine,

while the distant horizon
dwarfs a mountain
to a grain.

There, lay down
your demons to rest,
at the foot of this mountain.

This Emerald

Now all of summer's days have fallen
off the calendar, and early October
infuses waning sun rays sinking

within the skin a feeling's
last concentrated core
heat reminding of its absence

for months to come; how age
slowly works, its numb
narcotic doesn't weaken,

and we don't waken. No wonder
we say "Enter" to another
predictable terrible day,

extinction raping
continually the climate
of our later reaping.

What if might have been
could have been flourished in, like
the frightful, fruitful confusions

of creation? All those sins
turned in for their sexy
twins; the way happiness wins,

at times, by risking the instant chance
of its opposite, like a cleansing
wind caught in a trance

of slowness,
slow, motion-
less;

how intuition senses ways of going
forward with only hints
of knowing, like Pollock continuing

pure feeling without losing
momentum from edge
to edge, not stopping.

Not just a leap—
building a bridge
back after the leap!

Who will not need a house
of refuge when this emerald
garden is no oasis,

and summer withholds its golden
goblet, its green
mat of welcome.

Coffee House Press began as a small letterpress operation in 1972 and has grown into an internationally renowned nonprofit publisher of literary fiction, essay, poetry, and other work that doesn't fit neatly into genre categories.

Coffee House is both a publisher and an arts organization. Through our *Books in Action* program and publications, we've become interdisciplinary collaborators and incubators for new work and audience experiences. Our vision for the future is one where a publisher is a catalyst and connector.

LITERATURE
is not the same thing as
PUBLISHING

FUNDER ACKNOWLEDGMENTS

Coffee House Press is an internationally renowned independent book publisher and arts nonprofit based in Minneapolis, MN; through its literary publications and *Books in Action* program, Coffee House acts as a catalyst and connector—between authors and readers, ideas and resources, creativity and community, inspiration and action.

Coffee House Press books are made possible through the generous support of grants and donations from corporations, state and federal grant programs, family foundations, and the many individuals who believe in the transformational power of literature. This activity is made possible by the voters of Minnesota through a Minnesota State Arts Board Operating Support grant, thanks to the legislative appropriation from the arts and cultural heritage fund. Coffee House also receives major operating support from the Amazon Literary Partnership, the Bush Foundation, the Jerome Foundation, The McKnight Foundation, Target Foundation, and the National Endowment for the Arts (NEA). To find out more about how NEA grants impact individuals and communities, visit www.arts.gov.

Coffee House Press receives additional support from the Elmer L. & Eleanor J. Andersen Foundation; the David & Mary Anderson Family Foundation; the Buuck Family Foundation; the Carolyn Foundation; the Dorsey & Whitney Foundation; Dorsey & Whitney LLP; the Knight Foundation; the Rehael Fund of the Minneapolis Foundation; the Matching Grant Program Fund of the Minneapolis Foundation; the Schwab Charitable Fund; Schwegman, Lundberg & Woessner, P.A.; the Scott Family Foundation; the US Bank Foundation; VSA Minnesota for the Metropolitan Regional Arts Council; the Archie D. & Bertha H. Walker Foundation; and the Woessner Freeman Family Foundation in honor of Allan Kornblum.

THE PUBLISHER'S CIRCLE OF COFFEE HOUSE PRESS

Publisher's Circle members make significant contributions to Coffee House Press's annual giving campaign. Understanding that a strong financial base is necessary for the press to meet the challenges and opportunities that arise each year, this group plays a crucial part in the success of Coffee House's mission.

RECENT PUBLISHER'S CIRCLE MEMBERS INCLUDE

Many anonymous donors, Mr. & Mrs. Rand L. Alexander, Suzanne Allen, Patricia A. Beithon, Bill Berkson & Connie Lewallen, E. Thomas Binger & Rebecca Rand Fund of the Minneapolis Foundation, Robert & Gail Buuck, Claire Casey, Louise Copeland, Jane Dalrymple-Hollo, Ruth Stricker Dayton, Jennifer Kwon Dobbs & Stefan Liess, Mary Ebert & Paul Stembler, Chris Fischbach & Katie Dublinski, Kaywin Feldman & Jim Lutz, Sally French, Jocelyn Hale & Glenn Miller, the Rehael Fund-Roger Hale/Nor Hall of the Minneapolis Foundation, Randy Hartten & Ron Lotz, Jeffrey Hom, Carl & Heidi Horsch, Amy L. Hubbard & Geoffrey J. Kehoe Fund, Kenneth Kahn & Susan Dicker, Stephen & Isabel Keating, Kenneth Koch Literary Estate, Jennifer Komar & Enrique Olivarez, Allan & Cinda Kornblum, Leslie Larson Maheras, Lenfestey Family Foundation, Sarah Lutman & Rob Rudolph, the Carol & Aaron Mack Charitable Fund of the Minneapolis Foundation, George & Olga Mack, Joshua Mack, Gillian McCain, Mary & Malcolm McDermid, Sjur Midness & Briar Andresen, Maureen Millea Smith & Daniel Smith, Peter Nelson & Jennifer Swenson, Marc Porter & James Hennessy, Robin Preble, Jeffrey Scherer, Jeffrey Sugerman & Sarah Schultz, Nan G. & Stephen C. Swid, Patricia Tilton, Stu Wilson & Melissa Barker, Warren D. Woessner & Iris C. Freeman, Margaret Wurtele, Joanne Von Blon, and Wayne P. Zink.

For more information about the Publisher's Circle and other ways to support Coffee House Press books, authors, and activities, please visit www.coffeehousepress.org/support or contact us at info@coffeehousepress.org.

Fugitive, in Full View was designed by
Bookmobile Design & Digital Publisher Services.
Text is set in Adobe Caslon Pro.